BIBLE 202
THE STORY OF M

MW01121008

CONTENTS

Author: Iva Grant
Editor: Richard W. Wheeler, M.A. Ed.
Consulting Editor: W. Mel Alexander, Th.M., Ph.D.
Revision Editor: Alan Christopherson, M.S.

Alpha Omega Publications

300 North McKemy Avenue, Chandler, Arizona 85226-2618

ALPHA OMEGA
PUBLICATIONS

Learn with the Bridgestone characters:

When you see me, I will help your teacher explain the exciting things you are expected to do.

When you do actions with me, you will learn how to write, draw, match words, read, and much more.

You and I will learn about matching words, listening, drawing, and other fun things in your lessons.

Follow me and I will show you new, exciting truths, that will help you learn and understand what you study. Let's learn!

THE STORY OF MOSES

Hello _____ .
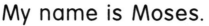
Print your name.

My name is Moses.
I am going to tell you a very exciting story.
This story began when I was a little baby.
God had something He wanted me to do.
You will see how God took care of me. You
will find out what He wanted me to do.
You will see what God is like.
He is like a father who can do anything.
You will see that God takes care of us. You
will see that God has a plan for us. You
will see that to obey God is good.
I hope you will like my story.

Objectives

Read these objectives. They tell you what you will be able
to do when you have finished this LIFEPAC.

1. You will be able to tell someone what God is like.

2. You will be able to name two things God does for you.

3. You will be able to tell someone about the story of
   Moses.

4. You will be able to write the name that God gave
   Himself when talking to Moses.

NEW WORDS

body (body). All of a person's or thing's parts.

bush. A large round plant.

bricks. Blocks made of mud.

destroy (de stroy). To get rid of. To bring to an end.

draw. To make a picture with a writing tool.

drove. Sent away.

Egypt (e gypt). The name of the country in which Moses lived.

heard. To hear something.

heavenly (heav en ly). Not part of the earth. Where God lives.

holy (ho ly). Something God has blessed.

maid. A helper in housework.

neither (nei ther). Not either one. Not any of the ones given.

nurse. One who takes care of people.

obey (o bey). To do what you are told.

path. A way made by people or animals walking.

spirit (spir it). God is a spirit person. He does not need to have a body like ours.

trembling (trem bling). Shaking.

verse. A small part of the Bible's writing.

voice. What you hear when someone speaks.

waded. Walked in water that is not deep.

These words will appear in **boldface** (darker print) the first time they are used.

I. EARLY LIFE OF MOSES

The first part of my story
is about my early life.
Many things happened to me.
Many things that happened to me
helped me learn things about God.
He took care of me by saving my life.
God had a plan for my life
and for His people.
God loved me.

WORDS TO STUDY

bricks		Blocks made of mud.
destroy	(de stroy)	To get rid of. To bring to an end.
draw		To make a picture with a writing tool.
Egypt	(e gypt)	The name of the country in which Moses lived.
heard		To hear something.
maid		A helper in housework.
nurse		One who takes care of people.
obey	(o bey)	To do what you're told.
verse		A small part of the Bible's writing.
waded	(wad ed)	Walked in water that is not deep.

People and Places

Goshen   Moses   Jewish

Ask your teacher to say these words with you.

Teacher Check _____

Note: Cut the **PICTURE WORD** list from the back of this LIFEPAC to use as you read this story.

THE HEBREW PEOPLE IN EGYPT

My [picture] and [picture] lived in Goshen. Goshen was a part of

Egypt. Our family had lived in Egypt for a very long time. They

took care of [picture] and were very happy.

The [picture] that loved my people was gone. A new [picture] took

his place. He did not like us. He wanted to get rid of us. He

called his [picture] to the [picture].

"We must do something about these people," said the [picture].

"There are too many of them. We are not safe. Make them work

very hard. We must get rid of them."

So the [picture] told the people they must work very hard.

"You must make **bricks** out of mud," the [picture] said.

My people worked very hard, but kept growing in numbers.

The [picture] was mad.

"There are too many of these people. They are too strong.

I have another plan to **destroy** them." he said

He called the into the  again.

The said, "Go to every . Take every baby

 and throw him in the river."

The walked up and down the streets. They went to

every . Everyone was afraid.

THE BABY MOSES

When my **heard** the , she took me and hid me.

My and loved God. They wanted me to grow up

to love God, too. My brother and my sister helped

keep me quiet. Someone stayed with me all the time. I did not

cry. The did not find me.

One day my said, "Baby Moses is too big to hide."

My and and wondered how they could help.

"What can we do?" they said.

Work the crossword puzzle.

Fill in the blanks. Print a word from the word box in each sentence. Use those words to do the puzzle.

1.1 **ACROSS**

1. They made _____ out of mud.

2. We live in a _____ .

3. The king lives in a _____ .

DOWN

4. My mother _____ me.

5. They took care of _____ .

6. The people worked _____ .

When you have finished checking your work ask your teacher to check it with you. Put a star in the box for your good work.

| hard |
| bricks |
| house |
| hid |
| sheep |
| palace |

Teacher Check _____

 Put the number of the one who said it in the circle.
You may look in the story.

1.2 ◯ "You must make bricks out of mud."

1.3 ◯ "This baby is too big to hide."

1.	king
2.	soldiers
3.	mother

1.4 ◯ "We must do something about these people."

1.5 ◯ "Take every baby boy and throw him in the river."

When your answers are right put a star in the box. ☐

 had another plan. She said, "Miriam and I will go down

to the river and get some tall grass. We will make a nice

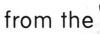. Then you will see what we can do to save Moses

from the . We must make this  very strong,"

 said. "It will float on the ."

When the  was finished, she put a soft

in it. Mother put me on the in the .

"God will take care of you," she whispered softly.

page 7 (seven)

Trace the letters of the sentence.

1.6

God loves me.

Read the sentence.

1.7   Is the sentence true?   **Write** yes **or** no. _____

 picked up the . "Come with me,"

she said to . Down the  they walked carrying me in the

 . They soon came to the  . took the

 and carefully put it on the . Then quietly

hid nearby.

    The floated on the . My was so

nice and soft. I went to sleep.

    When I woke up I heard laughing and talking. The

had come to the river to take a bath. My knew that the

came everyday to take a bath. wanted the princess to find me.

Then I heard the say, "Look at that . Bring it to me."

 Read the sentence under the picture. **Draw** dot-to-dot. Follow the letters in the sentence. Start with **M**. Draw a line to **I**. Draw lines to the next letters until you come to the last letter. When you are finished, color the basket.

Miriam **watched the basket.**

1.8   What did you draw? I drew a _____ .

Her **maid waded** out in the water. She picked up the  and took it to the . "What is it? What is it?" she called. The looked in the  and saw me lying in my nice soft  . I was crying.

 Choose what you think will happen next.

1.9   What will the do next? Circle your answer.

a. She will put the basket back in the water.
b. She will keep the baby.
c. She will give him away.

Read to see what happens to Moses next. Were you right? If you were right, put a star in the box. ☐

The was surprised to see a baby. She picked me up. She held me close. "I love this baby." she said as she held me.

"I want to keep him. I will call him Moses." Then she cried sadly. "How can I take care of him. I am only a . I am not a mother."

ran to the from her hiding place in the nearby trees.

"I will get a **nurse** for you," she told the excitedly.

I was so happy when went to get my to be my

nurse. She brought to the .

The was pleased and asked, "Will you help me take

care of this baby? I will pay you for keeping him. When he is

bigger he will live with me."

My smiled as she took me in her arms. "I will take

good care of him," she said.

When I grew up, I remembered what happened to me. I

knew that God really loved me. God wanted me to do

something for Him and saved me from the .

How happy everyone was when we got home! prayed,

"Dear God, thank you for taking care of our baby. Amen."

 Draw a line under the one you choose.

1.10   How do you think felt when I was saved?

1.11   How do you think felt when I was saved?

1.12   God saved Moses from the soldiers.

    Yes   No

1.13   God takes care of little children so that when they grow up they can be God's helpers to His people.

    Yes   No.

 God takes care of you, too. He loves you. Close your eyes and thank God for taking care of you.

Learn this Bible verse.

We can read a **verse** in the Bible about little children. Ask your teacher to read it with you. Learn what Jesus said. Jesus said,

"Suffer the little children to come unto me, and forbid them not, for such is the kingdom of God." (Mark 10:14).

1.14   I would like for you to learn this verse. When You know the verse, say it to your teacher.

Teacher Check _____
                 Initial   Date

Put a star in the box when you have said it to your teacher. You will want to say it for your family, too. Look it up with them in your Bible at home. ☐

◄●●►

When I was a young boy, I found out that I would soon

have to live with the . I knew I would live in the  .

I wondered what it would be like. How would you feel if you

lived in the  ?

◄●●►

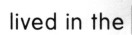

Finish this sentence.

1.15   If I lived with the princess I would _____

_____

_____

_____ .

page 13 (thirteen)

MOSES IN THE PALACE

I went to the [palace] to live. I was big enough to go to [school]. The [princess] princess loved me. She gave me a fine coat. I learned to read and write. I wrote on stones. I learned to do math. We also had [music] classes. I liked school.

At home in the palace, I listened to the [soldiers] talk. They talked about other countries. They talked about their [people].

I was always listening and learning.

I was growing up, too. Then one day the [king] chose me to head his [people]. I was glad I learned when I was a little boy growing up.

I loved the [princess]. I loved God. I loved my people. The [soldiers] were still mean to my people. One time I helped one of my people. Because of what I did, I knew I could not stay in the [palace].

I knew I must leave. I had to leave the . I thought that God must want me to live in another place. I said "Good-bye," and started down the to begin a new life.

- -

 Read the words on the stones. Find the words that belongs in the sentence. Write The word on the line.

help

God

music

school

listen

head

1.16   Moses went to live in the . He was big

enough to go to_____ .

1.17   In the [image] Moses went to_____ class.

1.18   Moses loved _____ .

1.19   Moses wanted to _____ his people.

1.20   Moses became _____ of an army.

1.21   Moses would _____ while the [image]
talked.

When you add the letter e to the end of a short word, the vowel becomes long and the e is silent.

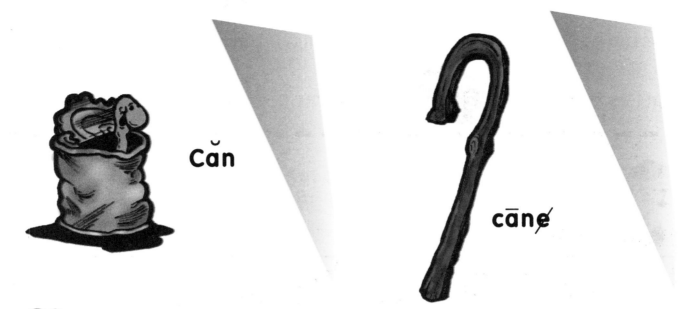

Că̆n

cāne̸

 Choose the correct word and write it in the blank for each sentence.

1.22   Mother said, "We will _____ Moses."

                    hid / hide

1.23   The Princess made Moses a beautiful _____.

                    rob / robe

1.24   Moses knew that God _____ all the stars.

                    mad / made

1.25   Moses _____ in the palace.

                 at / ate

1.26   The maid was told to _____ out in the water.

                  wad / wade

For the Self Test, study what you have read and done. The Self Test will check what you remember.

SELF TEST 1

Choose the best ending for the sentence. Draw a line to the answer. The first one is done for you.

The soldiers looked ———— from the soldiers.

1.01   Moses' family hid him   basket from tall grass.

1.02   Moses had a brother   for baby boys.

1.03   Moses' family made a   named Aaron.

1.04   Jesus loves   came to the river for
                                      a bath.

1.05   The princess   little children.

Put a circle around the right word to finish the sentence.

1.06   Miriam _____ by the river.
          lid   hid   rid

1.07   Moses _____ to live in the palace.
          with   want   went

1.08   The Hebrew people _____ in Egypt.
          lived   loved   laughed

1.09   In Egypt there was a new_____ .
          ring   king   thing

1.010   Moses' mother will _____ up the basket.

   peck   pick   poke

1.011   Moses was in a soft _____ .

   bid   bad   bed

1.012   The princess _____ the baby.

   held   help   hope

1.013   Miriam ran to _____ a nurse.

   gum   get   got

1.014   Moses would _____ to the soldiers.

   lesson   learn   listen

1.015   Moses will _____ the people.

   help   home   happy

Put a circle around the best ending to finish each sentence.

1.016   The princess wanted to _____ .

   keep the baby
   put the baby back
   give the baby to a soldier

1.017   The princess said she would pay the nurse to

   _____ .

   find a soldier
   take care of Moses
   come to the palace

1.018   Moses always _____.

loved God
was afraid
was angry

1.019   Moses wanted to _____.

go to the store
be the next king
help the people

  Teacher Check _____

My Score

II. MOSES IN THE DESERT

I hope you like the story of my life.
God is my Heavenly Father.
I talked to God.

In this part of my story,
you will see how God took care
of me again.
He gave me a new home.
God loved me.

WORDS TO STUDY

drove		Sent away.
heavenly	(heav en ly).	Not a part of earth. Where God lives.

Special Words

Jethro   Bible

Ask your teacher to say these words with you.

Teacher Check _____

JETHRO'S DAUGHTERS

I walked for many days.
I was all alone.
I had much time to think.
I thought about the princess.
I thought about my mother and father.
I thought about my people working so hard.
I wanted to see Aaron and Miriam.

At night I would find a good place
to lie down and sleep.
In the morning I would start walking again.

One day I saw something far away.
It looked like many sheep.
As I came closer, I saw some people.
Seven young girls were taking care
of their father's sheep. Their father's name
was Jethro. I was glad to see some people
again.

Write the words.
Moses saw plants like these. Each plant has
some hidden words. Match the top letters and
bottom letters. Write the new words on the lines.

la   ca   bu   se   mi   pu   de   ta   ri

_____ _____ mp   _____ _____ nt   _____ _____ sk

2.1 _____   2.4 _____   2.7 _____

2.2 _____   2.5 _____   2.8 _____

2.3 _____   2.6 _____   2.9 _____

Spell these short vowel words.

2.10   Write the words for each picture by spelling the ending.

j _ _ _ _ _ _ _

t _ _ _ _ _ _ _

m _ _ _ _ _ _ _

f _ _ _ _ _ _ _

p _ _ _ _ _ _ _

bl _ _ _ _ _ _

The girls came to the well
to get water for their sheep.
Sometimes unkind men
would bring their sheep to the well.
They would take the water
away from the girls.
Then the girls would have to get more water.

I saw the men being unkind to the girls,
so I made them go away.

BIBLE

2 0 2

LIFEPAC TEST

20 / 25

Name _____

Date _____

Score _____

BIBLE 202: LIFEPAC TEST

Answer Yes **or** No. **If the sentence is true circle** Yes. **If it is not true circle** No.

1. Yes   No   They hid the baby Moses.

2. Yes   No   The princess gave the baby away.

3. Yes   No   God wants children to come to Him.

4. Yes   No   Moses did not listen to the men talk.

5. Yes   No   Moses took care of sheep.

6. Yes   No   The people saw the ground burn up.

7. Yes   No   Moses saw a bush that did not burn up.

8. Yes   No   God said the ground was holy.

9. Yes   No   Moses could not hear God talking.

10. Yes   No   God wanted to help the people.

Number the sentences 1, 2, 3, **or** 4 **on the line to tell when each thing happened.**

11. _____   The bush was on fire.

12. _____   God talked to Moses.

13. _____   I will obey God.

14. _____   This is holy ground.

Choose the right word and write it in the sentence.

Bible   care   everywhere

God   loves   obey

plan   princess   rocks

spirit

15. God is _____ .

16. God took _____ of the baby.

17. Moses knew that _____ made everything.

18. God talks to us through the _____ .

19. God had a _____ for Moses.

20. Moses would look at the _____ and the mountains.

21. God _____ everyone.

22. Moses went to live with the _____ .

23. A _____ is something like the wind.

24. God wants us to _____ Him.

Finish this sentence.

25. I love God because _____

_____ .

NOTES:

The girls were thankful
because they were able to water their sheep.
When they returned home early,
their father asked,
"Why are you home so soon?"
"We are home early,
because a man helped us.
He **drove** the men away.
He helped us get water, too," they answered.
"Where is the man now?" the father asked.
"Go and find him. I want to thank him."
The girls obeyed and went looking for me.
The girls found me.
They asked if I would go with them.
They were kind to me.
The father asked me to work for him.
I could live in their house.
I would take care of some of the sheep.

 Check (✓) the best name.

2.11   What is a good name for this story?
   ☐ Moses Walked a Long Time
   ☐ Moses Sent the Men Away
   ☐ Moses Finds a New Home

Tell your teacher why you chose this answer.

Teacher Check _____
                          Initial   Date

Circle the best word for the sentence.

2.12   Moses was _____ to the girls with the sheep.
           kind   mean   unfair

2.13   The girls' father wanted to _____ Moses.
           leave   thank   pay

2.14   The girls were _____ that Moses was
           kind to them.
           careful   skillful   thankful

MOSES' NEW FAMILY

I was happy with Jethro's family.
I liked one of those girls.
I thought she was pretty.
I knew that I loved her,
and she became my wife.
God gave us a baby boy.
We were happy.

I took care of the sheep.
Sometimes I had to find
a new place for my home,
because my sheep needed more green grass.

While I was walking
by myself with the sheep,
I talked to God.
I knew God was with me.
I knew God when I was a little boy.
He was with me in the palace.

While I was watching the sheep
I knew He was with me.
I was so happy that God was EVERYWHERE,
and He was ALWAYS with me.

Learn a Bible verse.

God was with Moses. God is with us, too.
Print your name in the verse.

_____ , "I will be with thee."

(Exodus 3:12)

Learn this verse. When you know it, say it for your
teacher. Put a star in the box when you have learned
the verse.

Teacher Check _____

Initial   Date

GOD'S BEAUTIFUL WORLD

   While the sheep were eating,
I would look around.
I had to watch for animals
that would kill the sheep.
   I would watch the bugs on the ground.
I would look at the rocks.
I would pick up pretty stones.
The birds would sing and fly over my head.
I would look at the tall mountains
and pretty trees.
I would think, "God made all of this!"
   I loved the nighttime.
I felt so close to God.
I looked up at the moon and the stars.
God made them all.
It was so beautiful.

 **Trace each white dot and you will see the "Big Dipper."**

"God made the world and all things therein . . ." (Acts 17:24).

Ask someone to help you find the "Big Dipper" in the night sky.

 Number the pictures.

2.15   Write the numbers 1, 2, 3, or 4 in the circle of the picture to tell when each thing happened.

Check your work. Put a star in the box for your good work.

 Teacher Check _____

Initial Date

Study what you have read and done for this Self Test. This Self Test will check what you remember of this part and other parts you have read.

SELF TEST 2

Write yes **or** no.

2.01 _____ Moses walked in the desert for many days.

2.02 _____ At first Moses saw no people in the desert.

2.03 _____ Obey means to send away.

2.04 _____ The girls' father was Jethro.

2.05 _____ Jethro chased Moses away from the well.

Match the word with the right phrase. Draw a line to the best answer.

2.06	heavenly	a.	sent away
2.07	Jethro	b.	talked with God in the desert
2.08	obey	c.	not earthly
2.09	drove	d.	had many daughters
2.010	Moses	e.	to do what you are told

2.011   Write the right word under each picture.

t _____

f _____

s _____

W _____

Circle the right word to finish the sentence.

2.012   Moses walked in the _____ for many days.

water   desert   snow

2.013   Moses saw many _____ at the well.

      sheep   dogs   birds

2.014   Unkind men would take the _____ away from the girls.

      sheep   food   water

2.015   The girls' father was named _____ .

      Jethro   Moses   Aaron

2.016   One of the girls became the _____ of Moses.

      friend   wife   mother

2.017   While Moses watched the sheep, he knew that God was _____ .

      everywhere   asleep   gone

16 / 20

Teacher Check _____
                 Initial   Date

My Score

III. MOSES AND THE BURNING BUSH

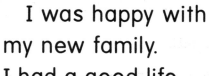

      I was happy with
my new family.
I had a good life.
I loved my family.
I liked my work.

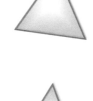

Taking care of sheep
made me feel close to God.
I looked at all the things God made.
I talked to God as I walked
with the sheep.
I saw God everywhere.
God was always with me.
He took care of me.
God saved me and gave me a good life.
He heard my prayers.
God wanted me to do something for Him,
so one day He talked to me.
The rest of my story is about God.

WORDS TO STUDY

body	(bod y)	All of a person's or thing's parts.
bush		A large round plant.
holy	(ho ly)	Something God has blessed.
neither	(nei ther)	Not either one. Not any of the ones given.
path		A way made by people or animals walking.
spirit	(spir it)	God is a spirit person. He does not need to have a body like ours.
trembling	(trem bling)	Shaking.
voice		What you hear when someone speaks.

Ask your teacher to say these words with you.

Teacher Check _____

GOD TALKED TO MOSES

I had been taking care of sheep
for a long time.
Sometimes I had to walk a long way
to find green grass for my sheep.
When I found a new place
with green grass, I would
stop there for the sheep.

One day the sheep were eating.
I was looking around
at the things God had made.
It was a nice place.
I rested.

Then something strange happened.
"What is that?
What is happening over there?"
I said as I jumped up.

There was a **bush** on fire! I walked closer.
I could see it burning. It was burning
but it did not burn up.
"Why doesn't that bush burn up?" I asked.

Then I heard someone call,
"Moses, Moses."

I answered, "Here I am."

"Moses take off your shoes
for this is **holy** ground," the **voice** said.
The voice was God speaking to me.

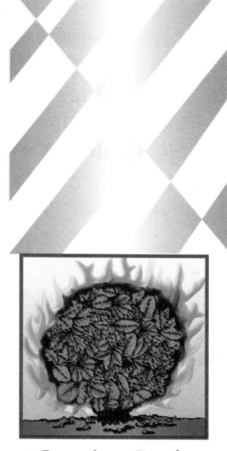

Burning Bush

I could not see God
but I could hear Him talk.
No one can see God
because He does not have a **body** like us.
God is everywhere.
God is a **spirit** person.
A spirit person does not need
to have a body like ours.

Because God is a spirit,
He comes to us in other ways.
He came to me in a bush that did not burn.

 **Read this poem with your teacher.** It will
help you know what a spirit is like. A spirit is
something like the wind.

WHO HAS SEEN THE WIND?

Who has seen the wind?
    Neither I nor you;
But when the leaves hang **trembling**,
    The wind is passing through.

Who has seen the wind?
    Neither you nor I;
But when the trees
    Bow down their heads,
The wind is passing by.
          by Christina Rossetti

 Teacher Check _____
                  Initial   Date

We cannot see the wind
but we know it is there.
We feel it on our faces.
Sometimes it makes us shiver.
We hear it swishing in the trees.
We see the wind blowing a kite in the sky.

We cannot see God.
We know He is there.
We see what He can do
in the flowers and trees.
We see His work in all the animals.

We know He keeps the world turning.
He gives us our hot and cold days.
He keeps the summer from getting too hot,
and He keeps the winter from getting too cold.
He wants to help us.
We know when He is living in our hearts.
We love God.
God loves us.
When we ask God to come into our hearts,
we **know** He is there.
God gives us a good life.

I was excited.
I had talked to God so many times.
Now God was talking to me.
I could hear His voice.
What did He want to tell me?

Write in the word from the list that best finishes the sentence. The first one is done for you.

Moses saw a burning ____**bush**____ .

3.1 God told Moses to take off his _____ .

3.2 God is a _____ .

3.3 We cannot see _____ .

3.4 A spirit is like the _____ .

3.5 When someone speaks, you hear his _____ .

3.6 God lives in our _____ .

wind
spirit person
God
voice
bush
shoes
hearts

He said, "I am God."
God said, "My people
are still working hard.
They have been praying to Me.
They are asking Me to help them."

It had been a long time
since I left Egypt.
I remembered how hard my people worked.
God still loved them and
wanted to help them.

God spoke some more.
He said, "I am going to take them
out of that land.
I am going to bring them
into a good land
where they will have better food."

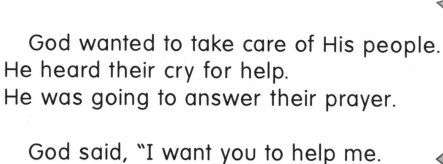

God wanted to take care of His people.
He heard their cry for help.
He was going to answer their prayer.

God said, "I want you to help me.
I want you to go to the palace and
talk to the king.
Tell him you want to take these people
out of Egypt."

Choose the right word. Put a circle around the word
that makes the sentence true. When your answers are
right put a star in the box.

God said:

3.7   "My people are still _____."

playing   working   running

3.8   "I hear them _____."

crying   laughing   talking

3.9   "I want to _____ them."

talk to   keep   help

3.10   "I want to bring them into a good _____."

palace   land   store

3.11   "I _____ these people."

want   forget   love

God spoke to Moses from the burning bush.
Does God ever speak to us?
How does He speak to us?
He speaks to us through
all the beautiful things we see.
Can you draw three pictures of things
God has made?

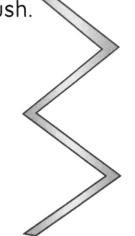

 Draw three things God has made.

3.12 God made these things.

Another way God speaks to us
is through the Bible.
In the Bible He tells us to love each other.
He tells us how to please Him.
He wants us to obey Him.
He wants us to read it everyday.
He wants us to learn some verses.

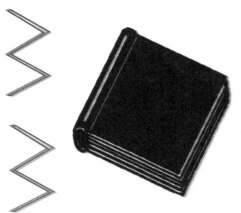

Learn this verse and say it to your teacher.

3.13   God said,

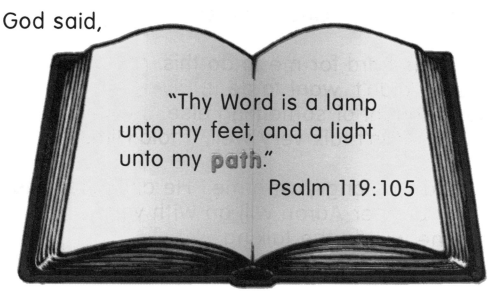

"Thy Word is a lamp unto my feet, and a light unto my **path**."

Psalm 119:105

Teacher Check _____

Initial   Date

MOSES TALKED TO GOD

God was telling me to go to the king
and ask him to let the people go.
God wanted me to go to the people.

God said, "Tell them
I will bring them out of Egypt."

I was afraid to do that.
I said, "I am not the man for that job."

But God said, "I will
be with you and help you."

"O God," I said,
"those people will not believe
that you sent me."

God answered, "Tell them that **I AM** has sent you."
I AM is one of God's names.

It was hard for me to do this.
I really didn't want to do it,
so I thought of something else.
"God, I don't talk very well," I told Him.

God was angry with me. He answered me,
"Your brother Aaron will go with you,
and he will do the talking."

Look in the story for the words. Write the word in the blank to finish each sentence. You will find the words in the story "Moses Talked to God" (page 37).

3.14   Moses did not want to go because

    a.   he was not the _____ for the job.

    b.   the people would not _____ him.

    c.   he did not _____ very well.

3.15   God answered,

    a.   "I will be _____ you."

    b.   "Tell them _____ has sent you."

    c.   "Your _____ will do the talking."

The bush had stopped burning,
God had stopped talking.
Everything was quiet.
I knew God loved my people.
I knew God had a plan for me.
I wanted to obey God.
God was good.

   I hope you liked my story.
I told you my story
so you can see that God talks to us
and wants to help us
if we pray to Him.
Later you will read about
the many great things God did
to help His people
leave the land of Egypt.

Here is a song about God for you to sing.

God Is So Good

1. God   is   so   good,   God   is   so   good,

    God   is   so   good, He's   so   good   to   me.

Verse Two
He cares for me,

Verse Three
I'll do His will,

Verse Four
He loves me so,

Write a word that tells what the picture is.
Spell the endings of the words. (Hint: Use a word
that ends in a silent e.)

3.16

s _____

f _____

h _____

(not small)

h _____

c _____

r _____

Study what you have read and done for this last Self
Test. This Self Test will check what you remember in
your studies of all parts in this LIFEPAC. The last Self
Test will tell you what parts of the LIFEPAC you need to
study again.

SELF TEST 3

Circle the best word for the sentence.

3.01   Moses would look up at the _____ .

                stars   stamp

3.02   When Moses found green grass, he would _____ _____ there.

               stone   stop

3.03   We hear the wind swishing in the _____ .

               trees   trucks

3.04   The wind is _____ .

               blowing   blue

3.05   God will _____ the people to a good land.

               brag   bring

Find the word that belongs in the sentence. Use these words.

       us   /   on   /   AM   /   asked   /   else

3.06   I _____ sent Moses to help his people.

               (short a)

3.07   God gave _____ a baby boy.

               (short u)

3.08   The bush was _____ fire.

               (short o)

3.09   I thought of something _____ .

               (short e)

3.010   God _____ me to talk to the king.

               (short a)

$\frac{8}{10}$ Teacher Check _____

                         Initial   Date   **My Score**

Before taking the LIFEPAC Test, you should do these self checks.

1.   Did you do good work
     on your last Self Test?

2.   Did you study again those parts of the LIFEPAC
     you did not remember?

     Check one: ☐ Yes (good)
                       ☐ No (ask your teacher)

3.   Do you know all the new words in "Words to
     Study"?

     Check one: ☐ Yes (good)
                       ☐ No (ask your teacher)

PICTURE WORDS

Cut along this line.

 Aaron

 mother

 army

 music

 basket

 palace

 bed

 princess

 boy

 road

 father

 school

 house

 sheep

 king

 soldiers

 Miriam

 water

Cut along the dotted line and use this **PICTURE WORD** list as you read the first story.